This book is a work of nonfiction. While every effort has been made to ensure the accuracy of the information contained herein, certain names, dates, and events may have been condensed or summarized for clarity.

Published by Renegade Publishings

Designed in the United States of America

ISBN: 978-1-956088-13-7

First Edition: 2025

For inquiries, permissions, or bulk orders, contact:

Renegade Publishings

INTRODUCTION

This book is not a complete ledger of everyone who has stood up for democracy, justice, or truth. It is not a comprehensive encyclopedia of courage. Rather, it is a starting point—a curated set of profiles that shine a light on those who chose principle over comfort, truth over popularity, and action over silence.

The men and women featured in these pages are not all alike. They span the political spectrum. Some serve in government, others in the press, the courts, the streets, or the public eye. Some hold power; others confront it. But what unites them is a shared refusal to retreat when it would have been easier, safer, or more strategic to do so.

In recent years, the word *courage* has too often been used cheaply—to describe branding choices, partisan defiance, or viral moments. This book returns courage to its rightful context: as a moral and civic act performed in real time, under real risk, with consequences not just for the actor, but for the nation.

Many names are not included in this volume—not because they are unworthy, but because this work must begin somewhere. These 25 entries are a spark, not a conclusion. Each one invites readers to ask not only who else deserves to be remembered, but also: what does courage look like in our time? Who carries it now? And who will carry it next?

What follows is not mythology. It is documentation. It is a portrait of integrity under pressure, and a record of those who, when democracy needed them, did not look away.

Table of Contents

Nancy Pelosi
The Courage to Govern When Fear Is the Point

Title / Role: Speaker
Emeritus of the U.S. House of
Representatives
Term: 1987–present
Location: California
Education: BA, Trinity College
Party / Group: Democratic
Party

"Democracy bends only to law, not terror."

The Speaker stood in a secure location, surrounded by panic, fury, and uncertainty. Just moments before, rioters had breached the United States Capitol. The air outside was filled with tear gas. Inside, phones buzzed with unverified threats. Members of Congress huddled under chairs and behind walls. Staffers cried. Police officers bled.

And in the center of it all, Nancy Pelosi — Speaker of the House — made a quiet but irrevocable decision: the certification of the electoral vote would continue that night.

There was no press conference. No grand televised address. No symbolism. Just governance. In the middle of a democratic rupture, Pelosi reached not for drama but for duty.

Nancy Pelosi's courage was not born on January 6. It had been shaped over decades: through relentless attacks from political opponents, years of being caricatured, and her position as the most powerful woman in American politics. Her speakership was marked by opposition not just across the aisle but within her own party. She was often underestimated, sometimes ridiculed — but rarely outmaneuvered.

The violence that erupted on January 6 was personal. Pelosi was a central target. Rioters entered her office. Some called for her by name. But the threat didn't end with the mob. In the hours that followed, members of Congress floated arguments for delay, compromise, or procedural reconsideration — all veiled forms of appeasement.

Pelosi's refusal was absolute. Democracy, she argued, must not yield to intimidation — not from outsiders and not from within.

Pelosi's insistence on reconvening Congress that very night was not a political calculation. It was institutional discipline. Others may have waited, "out of caution." Pelosi knew that waiting would send a message: that fear works, that violence can distort timelines and temper resolve. Instead, she reminded the nation that the Constitution is not merely a document, but a responsibility — and responsibilities are not postponed for comfort.

This was not the first time she had chosen duty over popularity. Twice, she authorized impeachments of a sitting president, knowing both were likely to fail in the Senate. She did so not because they were politically advantageous — they were not — but because the acts demanded it. Accountability, in her view, was not about winning. It was about recording truth into the architecture of law.

Courage is often mistaken for charisma. But in a democracy, courage is continuity. It is the willingness to hold the line when others would redraw it. Nancy Pelosi's courage was procedural, deliberate, and ultimately invisible. She did not tweet it. She enacted it.

History will remember her for many things: her legislative victories, her influence on policy, her impact on the Democratic Party. But history must also remember the moment she kept the House together — not in a metaphorical sense, but literally. When walls were breached, she kept the chamber functioning.

And in doing so, she made an argument far more powerful than any speech: that democracy is not a performance. It is a process — and the most courageous act is simply not walking away.

Letitia James
The Courage to Enforce the Law When Power Pushes Back

Title / Role: New York Attorney General

Term: 2019–present
Location: New York City
Education: BA Lehman College, JD Howard University, MPA Columbia University

Party / Group: Democratic Party

"No one is above the law"

Letitia James knew from the beginning that enforcing the law against entrenched power would not make her popular — and might well make her a target. As the first Black woman to serve as New York Attorney General, she stepped into an office historically viewed as both a legal instrument and a political lightning rod. But James did not seek comfort. She sought accountability.

Her defining test came in the form of a civil investigation into one of the most politically volatile entities in America: the Trump Organization. From the moment she made her intentions clear, she became the subject of relentless attacks. Her motivations were questioned, her integrity challenged. In some corners of the press and the public, her office was painted as a political weapon.

But James remained focused. She understood that democratic law must be able to scrutinize not only the powerless, but the powerful. And if that scrutiny is abandoned in the face of intimidation, then democracy is reduced to a stage play — power unchecked by accountability.

Her investigation was not hasty. It was meticulous. James oversaw years of data collection, testimony, and forensic analysis. She avoided grandstanding. She let the facts speak. In an age when political messaging too often overwhelms institutional integrity, she made the institution matter.

The courage Letitia James displayed was not rhetorical. It was procedural. In pressing a civil case based on financial misrepresentation and systemic fraud, she affirmed something Americans had begun to doubt: that the law can still reach upward. That justice can still apply even when wealth, media, and influence stand in its way.

She faced backlash not just from political opponents, but from institutional inertia — the subtle pressure to wait, delay, or avoid conflict altogether. But for James, justice delayed was justice surrendered.

Her pursuit of accountability reminded Americans that the promise of equal justice is only meaningful if it is enforced when it is hardest to do so. James helped restore public faith in regulatory mechanisms by showing that they could still function, still push back, still draw lines.

Her work was a reminder that courage in law is often quiet, sustained, and unglamorous. It is not always dramatic courtroom scenes or public showdowns. It is paperwork. It is subpoenas. It is trust in process.

But it is also resistance to fear. To power. To inertia.

Letitia James brought courage to the role not by stepping outside the law, but by staying inside it — when staying inside required standing.

Gavin Newsom
The Courage to Lead Amid Crisis

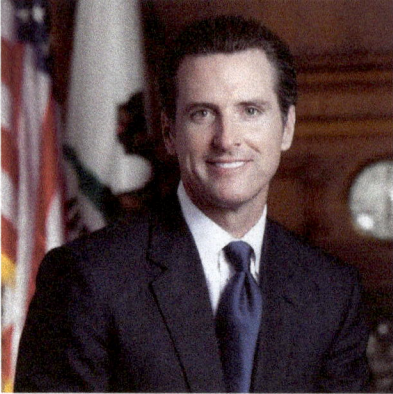

Title / Role: Governor of California
Term: 2019–present
Location: California
Education: BA Santa Clara University
Party / Group: Democratic Party

"California is not the exception — we're the rule for what's possible in democracy."

In a nation increasingly fractured by crisis and partisanship, Gavin Newsom stood at the helm of the largest, most diverse state in the union—and chose to govern not by calculation, but by conviction. At a moment when risk aversion was the political norm, Newsom made decisions that risked his own popularity in defense of public health, civil liberties, and democratic ideals.

When COVID-19 struck, California was one of the first states to shut down. It was a move that drew swift condemnation from opponents and uncertainty from residents. The stakes were massive: a collapsed economy, a restless public, and daily lives upended. But Newsom moved decisively, guided not by political polling but by epidemiology and the moral obligation to save lives.

He issued sweeping stay-at-home orders. He deployed the National Guard for humanitarian aid. He defended science in the face of disinformation and political attacks. His briefings were measured, unflinching, and often lonely. He knew the economic toll would be severe. He implemented rent relief and small business support while continuing to emphasize that democracy cannot function if public health collapses.

Yet Newsom's courage was not confined to the pandemic. As national courts stripped away reproductive rights, he turned California into a sanctuary. He signed legislation protecting abortion providers and patients, and allocated millions in funding to ensure access remained a right, not a privilege. He did so with the understanding that the fight was bigger than his state—it was about drawing a constitutional line in the sand.

He defended the rights of immigrants when federal policy sought to dehumanize them. He battled corporate utility giants over climate policy, even as wildfires ravaged the state. He resisted pressure to roll back environmental protections in the name of growth. And when critics called him extreme, he replied with data, resolve, and a clear understanding that boldness is often the precondition for justice.

Newsom survived a high-profile recall effort—one backed by misinformation and political resentment—because voters recognized something fundamental: he was governing with principle under fire. He didn't shy away from scrutiny. He leaned into it. And that transparency, even when flawed or imperfect, reflected democratic courage.

In an era when many leaders chased consensus, Newsom stood for something else: coherence. The belief that policy, even under duress, must be grounded in values—not volatility.

His statement—"California is not the exception — we're the rule for what's possible in democracy"—was not arrogance. It was aspiration. It reflected a faith that leadership, when accountable, courageous, and inclusive, can still offer a model for others to follow.

Gavin Newsom's courage lies in choosing action over inertia. In showing that, even in crisis, democracy can be not only preserved—but expanded.

Fani Willis

The Courage to Name Election Subversion

Title / Role: Fulton County District Attorney
Term: 2021–present
Location: Georgia
Education: BA Howard University, JD Emory University
Party / Group: Democratic Party

"Votes belong to the people"

Fani Willis never set out to be a national figure. She was a district attorney focused on her jurisdiction in Georgia, shaped by the daily realities of law and public service. But when democracy was strained by unprecedented attempts to overturn a presidential election, she did not hesitate. She treated it not as political theater but as a matter of criminal law.

Willis brought charges that reframed the events after the 2020 election not as mere controversy, but as a coordinated effort to subvert the will of the people. Her decision to investigate and prosecute these actions as crimes marked a shift: one that reminded Americans that votes are not abstractions—they are rights. And when rights are targeted, the law must act.

She faced intense pressure. Politicians and commentators questioned her motives. Threats poured in. Yet she stayed the course, driven not by partisanship, but by principle. She focused on the damage done to voters, to election workers, to the trust that undergirds the republic.

Her approach was methodical. She assembled a legal case that spoke in the language of justice, not ideology. Her narrative did not depend on headlines—it depended on facts, testimony, and statute. In doing so, she demonstrated that courage in public office is not loud; it is persistent.

Willis also elevated voices often forgotten in debates about democracy—those of local election workers like Ruby Freeman and Shaye Moss, who were targeted for doing their jobs. By seeking justice for them, she gave weight to the experiences of ordinary citizens facing extraordinary intimidation.

Her courage reminded Americans that laws are not meant to sit idly by while democracy is threatened. They are tools—and those who wield them must do so with clarity, even under duress. She made clear that criminality cloaked in politics is still criminality.

In holding the line, Fani Willis affirmed the principle that no one is above the law—not even those who once held the highest office. And by doing so, she restored a measure of faith in the machinery of justice.

Fani Willis did not dramatize her decisions. She simply did her job. And in times like these, that alone is an act of courage.

Adam Schiff
The Courage to Keep the Record

Title / Role: U.S. Senator / Former U.S. Representative, Chair of the House Intelligence Committee
Term: 2001–present
Location: California
Education: BA Harvard College, JD Harvard Law School
Party / Group: Democratic Party

"The truth matters even when it is inconvenient."

Adam Schiff didn't enter public life seeking a spotlight. He was a former federal prosecutor, precise and restrained by temperament, more attuned to fact than flourish. But in a political age increasingly dominated by spectacle, Schiff found himself in the most perilous role of all: the calm voice insisting that truth still matters — even when no one wants to hear it.

As Chair of the House Intelligence Committee, Schiff was tasked with leading one of the most consequential investigations in modern American history: foreign interference in the 2016 election and the conduct of a sitting president. The work would catapult him into national controversy. It would earn him enemies, threats, and mockery. Yet he never veered from the core idea that democracy depends on an accurate public record.

The obstacles he faced were not merely political. They were epistemological. In a time when truth itself was under assault —

dismissed as opinion, drowned in disinformation, weaponized against the very idea of accountability — Schiff chose to work slowly, deliberately, and with prosecutorial rigor. His hearings didn't always dominate the news cycle. They weren't designed to. They were designed to last.

The courage he displayed was not in exposing bombshells. It was in organizing facts that others wanted buried. Through countless hours of testimony, document review, and oversight hearings, Schiff worked to construct a ledger of democratic decline — a ledger that future generations could not ignore.

He faced derision on the House floor. He was caricatured by colleagues, insulted by the president, and threatened by angry citizens. His integrity was questioned, his patriotism maligned. But Schiff understood something few did: that impeachment was not just about removal. It was about history. About drawing a line so future officials would know where law and loyalty diverge.

Even when the outcome was foregone — when the Senate would not convict — Schiff still showed up, still argued, still documented. Not for political victory, but for constitutional fidelity.

In that sense, Schiff's courage was archival. He preserved not only what happened, but how a democracy responded to it. He ensured that the machinery of oversight did not rust from neglect. And in doing so, he gave the country something more valuable than scandal: memory.

Schiff reminds us that democratic erosion doesn't happen all at once. It happens when no one bothers to notice, or worse, to record. By keeping the record — even when the system refused to act on it — Adam Schiff performed one of the most essential tasks of democracy: witness.

Eric Holder
The Courage to Expand Justice

Title / Role: U.S. Attorney General
Term: 2009–2015
Location: Washington, D.C.
Education: BA Columbia College, JD Columbia Law School
Party / Group: Democratic Party

"The arc of the moral universe does not bend toward justice unless we help it bend."

Eric Holder became the first African American to serve as Attorney General of the United States, but his courage was defined not by that historic first—it was defined by what he chose to do with the role once he had it.

When he stepped into office in 2009, the Department of Justice was still reeling from years of politicization. Confidence in the impartiality of law enforcement had eroded. Holder understood that restoring that trust meant confronting some of the most entrenched and uncomfortable legacies of American power: voter suppression, systemic racism, and the fragility of civil liberties under stress.

He did not flinch.

Holder made voting rights a cornerstone of his tenure. At a time when states began introducing restrictive laws in the name of "integrity," Holder called them what they were—efforts to suppress the votes of minorities, the elderly, and the poor. He led legal challenges against voter ID laws and redistricting schemes that diluted Black and brown political power. His Justice Department blocked discriminatory measures and reminded the nation that access to the ballot is not a regional privilege—it is a constitutional right.

But his pursuit of justice went deeper. Under his leadership, the DOJ launched investigations into police departments with records of abuse, from Ferguson to Cleveland. He pushed for sentencing reform, calling out the devastating human toll of mandatory minimums and mass incarceration. He spoke openly, and often, about the racial disparities that defined the American justice system—not as a flaw to be ignored, but a wound to be acknowledged and treated.

His critics called him radical, activist, even un-American. But Holder made clear that defending the rule of law includes defending the people the law has too often failed. He was not content with maintaining order—he demanded fairness.

In moments of national crisis—after mass shootings, racial violence, and political gridlock—Holder insisted that the Department of Justice be a moral actor, not just a procedural one. He took positions that were legally sound and politically risky. He spoke plainly when silence would have been easier. He bore the weight of political attack, knowing that reform without resistance is impossible.

Even after leaving office, Holder's courage did not recede. He led national efforts to end gerrymandering, to protect the courts, and to defend democratic norms under threat. His post-government work made clear that public service does not end with the title—it endures in action.

His words—"The arc of the moral universe does not bend toward justice unless we help it bend"—were not rhetorical. They were a mandate. Holder believed the law is not static, but a living instrument—and if it is not made more just, it becomes a tool of injustice.

Eric Holder's courage was legal, moral, and deeply personal. He did not only uphold the law. He tried to elevate it.

Mark Kelly

The Courage of Public Service After Personal Loss

Title / Role: U.S. Senator, Former Astronaut
Term: 2020–present (Senate); NASA Astronaut: 2001–2011
Location: Arizona
Education: BS U.S. Merchant Marine Academy, MS Naval Postgraduate School
Party / Group: Democratic Party

"Courage means standing up when it's hard, not just when it's easy."

Mark Kelly's journey into public life did not begin with ambition—it began with tragedy. In January 2011, his wife, Congresswoman Gabrielle Giffords, was shot in the head during a constituent event in Tucson, Arizona. Six people were killed. The nation watched in horror, and for many, it would have been the end of a chapter.

For Kelly, it was the beginning of another.

Up until that moment, he had already lived a life shaped by courage: as a Navy combat pilot flying missions in Operation Desert Storm, as a NASA astronaut completing four spaceflights, and as part of the only sibling pair to travel beyond Earth. His was a résumé etched in risk, discipline, and exploration. But it was what came next—the work after the trauma—that would define his civic courage.

Kelly could have remained a private citizen. He had earned that right. Instead, he stepped forward into one of the most emotionally charged and politically divisive issues in American life: gun safety. Alongside Giffords, he co-founded an organization dedicated to reforming gun laws and reducing violence—not with rage, but with relentless focus and moral clarity.

He entered the debate not with slogans, but with the weight of lived experience. And in doing so, he reframed the conversation from ideology to humanity. For Kelly, this was not about partisanship. It was about responsibility. He met with lawmakers, law enforcement, and communities torn apart by gunfire. He listened, advocated, and reminded America that courage after pain is not reactive—it is constructive.

In 2020, Kelly ran for Senate in Arizona, a battleground state where moderation is prized and polarization is high. He ran as someone who had seen the worst of political violence and still believed in the best of democracy. He didn't promise easy answers. He promised commitment. And he won.

As a senator, Kelly has focused on issues ranging from national security and veterans' health to infrastructure, climate resilience, and restoring bipartisan functionality to a paralyzed chamber. He is not the loudest voice in the room—but often, he is the most grounded. His service is defined by pragmatism, by an engineer's precision, and by a survivor's sense of purpose.

"Courage means standing up when it's hard, not just when it's easy." That belief echoes through his votes, his speeches, and his quiet refusal to treat democracy as performance. He does not wear his heroism on his sleeve. He embodies it in consistency.

Mark Kelly's courage is not cinematic. It is constitutional. He chose to step into public life not out of calculation, but because the system needed voices that had known both gravity and grief—and still believed the future could be better.

He traded the vastness of space for the turbulence of politics—not because it was safer, but because it was necessary.

Michael McFaul
The Courage to speak Truth Abroad and at Home

Title / Role: U.S. Ambassador to Russia
Term: 2012–2014
Location: Moscow, Russia / United States
Education: BA Stanford University, DPhil Oxford University
Party / Group: U.S. Diplomatic Corps

"Diplomacy is not just negotiation — it is standing for values under pressure."

Diplomacy, at its best, is not the art of appeasement, but the courage to stand for truth amid silence and surveillance. In one of the most difficult geopolitical assignments of the modern era, Michael McFaul brought not only a deep knowledge of Russia to his role as U.S. Ambassador—but a moral compass calibrated toward democracy, even when the winds blew violently in the opposite direction.

Appointed during a period of rapidly deteriorating U.S.-Russia relations, McFaul entered his post in Moscow under a shadow. He was not a career diplomat. He was a scholar, a democracy advocate, and someone Russian officials viewed with open suspicion. Almost immediately, the pressure began. State media vilified him. Protesters followed his motorcade. His meetings were surveilled and distorted in propaganda. He was called a revolutionary, a spy, a threat to the Russian state.

But McFaul did not retreat.

Rather than try to win favor with the Kremlin through silence, he met openly with opposition leaders and civil society groups. He supported human rights defenders and used his platform to elevate voices critical of Vladimir Putin's growing authoritarianism. In doing so, he redefined the role of ambassador—from that of a neutral emissary to a principled witness.

This approach was controversial, even within diplomatic circles. But McFaul believed diplomacy without values is just logistics. He saw the growing crackdown on dissent in Russia and chose to engage, not observe. He paid a price: constant security threats, relentless disinformation campaigns, and professional isolation from the regime he was sent to engage.

His courage extended beyond his time in Moscow. After returning to the United States, McFaul became one of the most prominent public critics of Putin's regime, warning about authoritarian influence long before it became a mainstream concern. He challenged conventional wisdom in foreign policy circles, arguing that the United States could not ignore moral dimensions in its relationships with authoritarian powers.

When Russia invaded Ukraine, McFaul was one of the clearest and most consistent voices explaining the stakes—not only for Europe, but for global democracy. He did not just analyze. He advocated—for sanctions, support, and moral clarity.

He also became a target. Russian authorities issued a warrant for his arrest. Troll farms and state-sponsored media continued to smear him. Yet he remained firm, translating decades of academic work into urgent calls for action. He reminded Americans that international politics is not distant—it is deeply tied to the health of our own democracy.

"Diplomacy is not just negotiation — it is standing for values under pressure." McFaul lived that ethos, even when standing meant standing alone.

Michael McFaul's courage lies in his refusal to normalize repression. In an era when diplomacy often favors discretion, he chose transparency. In a role designed for tact, he practiced truth. His voice remains, not just as a former ambassador, but as a modern conscience in the global fight for democratic integrity.

J.B. Pritzker
The Courage to Govern with Equity

Title / Role: Governor of Illinois
Term: 2019–present
Location: Illinois
Education: BA Duke University, JD Northwestern University
Party / Group: Democratic Party

"Government should not be a barrier to justice — it should be a bridge."

J.B. Pritzker didn't campaign as a culture warrior. He campaigned as a problem solver. Yet when democracy began to fray under pressure and regression disguised itself as tradition, he governed with unmistakable moral clarity.

As Governor of Illinois, Pritzker has proven that courage in leadership isn't always loud—but it is always unflinching. His tenure has been marked by a steady, inclusive vision of government not merely as a regulator, but as a force for justice and dignity in people's lives.

When reproductive rights were under siege across the country, Pritzker made Illinois a fortress of freedom. He signed legislation codifying the right to choose into state law and eliminated outdated restrictions that obstructed access. While courts elsewhere turned backward, he expanded protections and doubled down on the belief that autonomy is not negotiable.

His courage extended beyond the courtroom. In mental health—long a neglected pillar of public policy—he launched the largest expansion of behavioral health care in Illinois history. He called for a transformation in how states fund, deliver, and destigmatize mental health services. Where past leaders had deferred action, he brought urgency.

Pritzker's equity agenda also took root in economic policy. He championed reforms to the state's tax structure, invested in early childhood education, and directed funding to historically underserved communities. His administration sought to close gaps not only in wealth, but in opportunity. He believed justice isn't only about civil rights—it's about the conditions that allow people to thrive.

All of this came at a time when governing boldly could have cost him politically. Illinois, while blue in national elections, is no stranger to ideological divides. His opponents framed equity efforts as overreach, but Pritzker held his course—not with combative rhetoric, but with evidence, consistency, and deeply held values.

"Government should not be a barrier to justice — it should be a bridge." That line, delivered without flourish, defines his leadership philosophy. He has turned his office into a tool for inclusion, not inertia.

Pritzker's courage is not only in what he supports—but in what he opposes. He resisted pressure to strip away trans rights, stood against book bans, and invested in education as a public good, not a partisan battleground. His vision of democracy is expansive, compassionate, and grounded in the everyday realities of people who are often left out of policy conversations.

In an era where loudness is often mistaken for leadership, Pritzker's methodical determination shows that courage can also be quiet, persistent, and pragmatic. His legacy—still unfolding—is not just about laws passed. It is about lives changed through governance that treats equity not as an aspiration, but as an obligation.

Jasmine Crockett
The Courage to Refuse Silence

Title / Role: U.S. Representative
Term: 2023–present
Location: Texas
Education: BA Rhodes College, JD
University of Houston
Party / Group: Democratic Party

"Silence is complicity."

Jasmine Crockett's entrance into the national political stage was neither quiet nor deferential. She arrived in Congress not as a career politician but as a former public defender — someone whose professional life had been defined by proximity to powerlessness, not privilege. Her voice, sharp with clarity and resistance, did not rise to seek attention. It rose because the silence around her was too loud to ignore.

From her first days in office, Rep. Crockett made it clear she would not participate in the performative decorum that often masks decay. She rejected the normalization of extremism, authoritarian rhetoric, and the false equivalency that cloaks political violence in the language of "both sides." In committee hearings, on the House floor, and across media platforms, she called out injustice with a precision born of courtroom discipline and lived experience.

Her courage has not been in volume, but in moral clarity. In an institution where young legislators — especially young Black women — are often expected to temper their tone to be taken seriously, Crockett did the opposite. She sharpened her language, naming what others danced around. She understood that euphemism is how institutions justify inertia. And inertia, in the face of democratic decline, is complicity.

She has faced dismissal, mockery, and barely veiled attempts to marginalize her. Yet she has persisted — not just by speaking out, but by reshaping the very conversation. Crockett does not posture. She prosecutes — with facts, with fire, with a refusal to let democratic backsliding become background noise.

Her presence is not merely symbolic. It is a reminder that representative democracy must include those who live closest to the consequences of its failures. Her voice resonates because it is rooted in service, not status.

In defending truth, she also defends belonging. Crockett speaks not only for herself, but for a generation raised in disillusionment — a generation that has seen democracy teeter and has refused to let it fall quietly. Her message is simple but profound: silence is not neutrality. It is surrender.

And in refusing to be silent, Jasmine Crockett offers a blueprint for how democracies endure — not through politeness or patience, but through principled confrontation with what must not be allowed to stand.

CHAPTER II — Military & National Security Courage

James Mattis
The Courage to Break Silence

Title / Role: U.S. Secretary of Defense
Term: 2017–2019
Location: United States
Education: BA Central Washington
University, MA National War College
Party / Group: Independent

"We must reject contempt for the Constitution."

James Mattis built a career on duty, discipline, and silence. Known by the call sign "Mad Dog," he was a revered military leader — blunt, deeply read, and unwavering in his fidelity to the armed forces. But in retirement, Mattis found himself facing a different kind of test: not how to lead troops in war, but how to defend the Constitution from within civilian life, when the threat came not from abroad but from within.

As Secretary of Defense under President Donald Trump, Mattis sought to act as ballast. He believed deeply in the apolitical nature of the military and resisted attempts to draw the Department of Defense into partisan conflict. But even ballast has limits. In 2019, when the President's impulses ran counter to the foundational principles of civilian control, international alliances, and constitutional governance, Mattis resigned.

What came after was more unexpected. For nearly a year, he remained silent, adhering to the traditional code of former military leaders. But then came June 2020.

When peaceful protestors were forcibly cleared from Lafayette Square so that President Trump could stage a photo at St. John's Church, Mattis saw a red line crossed — the use of military force to suppress domestic dissent for the sake of political optics. And he spoke.

His words cut with surgical precision: "We must reject contempt for the Constitution." It was a rebuke not only of one act, but of a growing authoritarian rhetoric that threatened democratic guardrails. Coming from a figure so deeply respected by conservatives and military institutions, Mattis's statement carried immense weight. It reminded the public that the military's loyalty is to the Constitution — not to a man.

Mattis faced predictable backlash. Critics on the right accused him of betrayal. But he did not respond with polemics or partisanship. His was the courage of restraint — a refusal to engage in the political fray, but a willingness to speak when silence would imply consent.

What made Mattis's statement so profound was not its volume but its timing. He waited until it mattered most — when silence would have been seen as complicity. And when he spoke, he did so with the moral clarity of a man who had spent a lifetime defending the republic, both in combat and at home.

In a democracy, courage sometimes means breaking your own code. For James Mattis, the decision to speak out — after decades of disciplined silence — became one of his most patriotic acts. It was a reminder that loyalty to country must always transcend loyalty to office.

H. R. McMaster
The Courage to Defend Truth

Title / Role: National Security Advisor
Term: 2017–2018
Location: United States
Education: BA United States Military Academy, PhD University of North Carolina at Chapel Hill
Party / Group: U.S. Military

Strategic competence requires truth."

"

Few national security officials have had to navigate as treacherous a political landscape as Lieutenant General H. R. McMaster. A decorated combat veteran and a scholar of military history, McMaster stepped into the role of National Security Advisor in 2017 with one goal: to restore the primacy of truth in American decision-making.

From the moment he entered the West Wing, McMaster found himself in a war of narratives. Intelligence was being filtered through political ideology. Facts were subverted by agendas. The very apparatus designed to inform and protect the presidency was at risk of becoming a tool for misinformation. McMaster knew this danger intimately — he had studied it in authoritarian regimes, written about it in military doctrine, and now, he was living it.

His courage lay not in confrontation but in constancy. He refused to allow classified intelligence to be cherry-picked for headlines or distorted to serve a personal narrative. He insisted on strategic clarity, even when it clashed with presidential preference. And he paid the price.

McMaster clashed repeatedly with senior White House figures over the role of the intelligence community and the sanctity of facts. He refused to bend assessments to fit politics. He defended allies when the president attacked them. He stood by the intelligence professionals under his watch, even as trust in their work was publicly undermined.

The obstacles were immense. Leaks undermined him. Allies in the administration turned on him. And eventually, he was replaced — not because he failed, but because he succeeded in reminding too many people of truths they preferred to ignore.

Yet McMaster never retaliated. After his departure, he remained loyal to the institution of national security — not to any party or figure. In his public remarks and writings, he championed the idea that democracies survive only when their leaders are grounded in truth. That competence — real competence — requires clarity, honesty, and a commitment to evidence.

His stance mattered not only for what it preserved, but for what it prevented. In an era of global disinformation and strategic instability, McMaster's insistence on truth created a firewall between the intelligence community and the creeping threat of authoritarian-style distortion.

In defending the integrity of intelligence, McMaster was defending something larger — the idea that democratic decisions must be built on facts, not feelings; on truth, not tantrum. His courage was intellectual, institutional, and deeply moral.

H. R. McMaster may be remembered as a scholar-general. But history may also remember him as something quieter, and rarer: a man who refused to lie when lies were in fashion.

Retired Generals and Admirals
The Courage of Collective Warning

Title / Role: Retired Senior
Military Leaders
Term: 2021 (Public Intervention)
Location: United States
Education: Various
Party / Group: U.S. Armed
Forces

"Support and defend the Constitution."

Courage is often imagined as individual. But in 2021, it arrived as a chorus—measured, deliberate, and unmistakably clear. A group of over 120 retired generals and admirals, men and women who had spent lifetimes in uniform, stepped back into public life not to reclaim influence, but to issue a warning. Their message was aimed at the very institution they once led: the United States military. And it carried the weight of history.

Their open letter reminded every active-duty service member of their true oath—not to any president or political party, but to the Constitution itself. It was a striking move: senior military figures, long committed to silence and neutrality in civilian politics, choosing instead to speak with unified voice at a moment when democratic norms were visibly fraying.

They did not issue threats. They issued principles. And those principles mattered because they came from experience. These were leaders who had commanded troops in battle, advised presidents in crisis, and seen up close what happens when militaries forget their role in a democracy.

The timing of the letter was no accident. It came in the wake of a presidential election marred by false claims, insurrection, and efforts to co-opt the language of patriotism for undemocratic ends. It was clear that the line between political loyalty and military obedience had grown dangerously thin. The retired officers saw that thinness—and decided to thicken it, with truth.

They reminded the military rank and file that illegal orders must be refused. That the strength of the armed forces comes not just from weapons or strategy, but from moral restraint. That their role is not to serve the ambitions of any one leader, but to protect the framework that allows leaders to rise and fall peacefully.

It was a moment of institutional self-defense—not for themselves, but for the republic. In a polarized era, when nearly every public gesture is interpreted through partisan lens, these officers chose the Constitution as their only allegiance. And in doing so, they offered Americans something rare: a demonstration that courage can still be collective.

They faced criticism from both extremes. Some questioned their motives; others saw their silence in earlier years as complicity. But their message was not retrospective. It was forward-facing. It was meant for those still wearing the uniform, facing impossible decisions in a destabilized political climate.

Their courage was the courage of elders—not to command, but to warn. Not to intervene, but to remind. In doing so, they fulfilled the final responsibility of leadership: to leave behind a trail of clarity for those who follow.

The oath, they said, is to the Constitution. And if that truth ever needs defending again, it will be ready—carried forward by those who once led, and still watch.

CHAPTER III — Courts, Judges, and Legal Courage

Federal Judges Blocking Executive Actions
The Courage to Rule Against Power

Title / Role: Federal Judiciary
Term: 2017–2021
Location: United States
Education: Law degrees (various)
Party / Group: Federal Judiciary

"The Constitution is not optional."

In the separation of powers, the judiciary is often imagined as the quiet branch. But between 2017 and 2021, a group of federal judges across the United States became something else: a bulwark. Not against a political party, but against the erosion of constitutional limits.

These judges — appointed by presidents of both parties — did not seek to be part of a resistance or a revolution. They acted, case by case, on the principle that no individual, regardless of office, is above the law. And when executive actions exceeded legal authority, violated constitutional protections, or ignored due process, they did what democracy requires of its courts: they said no.

The stakes were not theoretical. Some rulings involved immigration bans that targeted religion or nationality. Others dealt with the rollback of civil rights protections, attempts to bypass congressional authority, or efforts to intimidate whistleblowers and suppress dissent. These judges knew their rulings would not be popular in certain circles. They knew they could become targets of social media rage, political denunciation, or even threats to their safety. Yet they ruled anyway — not because of ideology, but because of oath.

The courage of the judiciary in this era was procedural, not performative. Decisions came not with soundbites, but with citations. Judges leaned on precedent, constitutional text, and the logic of checks and balances. Some wrote fiery dissents. Others issued narrow injunctions. But together, their rulings formed a critical truth: that democratic governments are bound by law, even when tempted by power.

What made these moments so vital was the context. In an environment where norms were being tested and institutions pressured to conform, the judiciary chose friction. They did not defer to the executive out of habit or fear. They insisted on scrutiny, transparency, and limitation — the very things the judiciary exists to provide.

Their rulings did not stop all abuses. They did not reverse every policy. But they preserved a constitutional record and held space for future remedies. In doing so, they reminded the nation that the law is not an instrument of the powerful. It is the defense of the governed.

Some judges acted alone, issuing emergency injunctions in the middle of the night. Others joined panels and appellate courts, crafting majority opinions that would stand for generations. What united them was not politics, but courage — the willingness to place the Constitution above convenience, and principle above pressure.

In an age when political branches strained against restraint, the judiciary became the last line of defense. And the judges who stood their ground — even quietly, even briefly — carried forward the enduring idea that democracy does not function without referees willing to call a foul.

Their message, written in the margins of law books and federal rulings, was unambiguous: The Constitution is not optional.

Supreme Court Justices (Dissents)
The Courage to Preserve the Law

Title / Role: Associate Justices of the
 Supreme Court
Term: Various
Location: United States
Education: Law degrees (various)
Party / Group: Judicial Branch

"Dissent speaks to the future."

Not all courage lies in victory. In the highest court of the United
States, some of the most important voices in defense of the
Constitution have been those in the minority—writing not for the
present, but for posterity. These are the justices whose dissents,
often overlooked in the moment, have preserved the moral and legal
foundations upon which democracy rests.

To dissent on the Supreme Court is not simply to disagree. It is to
stand against the tide of institutional consensus, often in moments
when public sentiment and political pressure push hard in the
opposite direction. It is a lonely form of conviction, where the writer
knows that their view will not carry the day, but may carry the truth
into the future.

Throughout recent years, dissenting opinions from justices such as
Sonia Sotomayor, Elena Kagan, and the late Ruth Bader Ginsburg

have articulated fierce defenses of voting rights, reproductive autonomy, equal protection, and the separation of powers. In these opinions, the justices did not merely catalog legal disagreements—they painted visions of what the law could and should be, grounded in history, constitutional fidelity, and human dignity.

When major rulings narrowed civil liberties or tilted power toward executive overreach, these dissents served as democratic ballast. They became the conscience of the Court. They reminded the public—and future courts—that the Constitution is a living framework, and that silence in moments of erosion is not neutrality, but surrender.

Their courage was often quiet, expressed through footnotes and legal citations, but its impact endures. Brown v. Board of Education was once a dissenting vision. So was Obergefell. So were many of the rights we now consider essential. Dissent is the seed of legal transformation.

These justices knew their positions might provoke backlash, that their words would be dissected and politicized. Still, they wrote. And in doing so, they left a trail of reason and resistance through moments of judicial compromise.

In times of democratic fragility, when precedent is overturned with haste and doctrine reshaped to match ideology, dissent becomes more than academic—it becomes a lifeline. It marks where the law was wounded, and where it might someday heal.

The phrase "Dissent speaks to the future" is not a platitude. It is a judicial act of hope. The hope that even when justice does not prevail today, it may be remembered—and restored—tomorrow.

CHAPTER IV — Journalism and Truth as Civic Defense

Rachel Maddow
The Courage to Explain Power

Title / Role: Journalist and Author
Term: 2008–present
Location: United States
Education: BA Stanford University, DPhil Oxford University
Party / Group: Independent Media

"History is how we see what is happening."

Rachel Maddow never set out to be a partisan warrior. Her power lies not in combat, but in coherence. In an age of noise, Maddow's courage has come from her insistence that understanding—not outrage—is the most powerful form of resistance.

Since 2008, Maddow has transformed the political talk show into something closer to a civic seminar. Night after night, she has used her platform not to shout, but to teach—to unspool complex histories, trace lines of authoritarian drift, and expose how erosion of norms begins quietly, in procedural shadows. Her signature style—carefully narrated, richly sourced, often historical—has become a lifeline for viewers trying to make sense of democratic decay in real time.

She does not simply report. She constructs narratives of power: how it operates, how it is abused, and how democracy unravels when its guardrails are stripped of memory. Maddow's historical analysis connects past to present, reminding her audience that what we are living through is not unprecedented—but that the consequences still can be.

This is not a safe or easy path in American media. Her deep dives into topics like the rise of fascism, judicial overreach, or corruption in foreign affairs often run counter to the instant-gratification ethos of modern news. Yet Maddow has remained unwavering. Her courage lies in refusing to simplify or sanitize. She trusts her audience to care about context.

She has faced criticism from all sides. Accused of alarmism by some, and not going far enough by others. But she has always returned to the same core principle: that democratic vigilance requires informed citizens. And informed citizens require history—not just headlines.

In times of democratic peril, Maddow's broadcasts have become a kind of emergency education. Not a call to arms, but a call to attention. She teaches the public how to recognize patterns, how to interpret shifts in language, how to see not just what is happening, but what it means.

This is what makes her more than a media figure. She is a civic interpreter. A translator of democratic crisis. Her voice has helped millions connect the dots—between disinformation and power, between law and abuse, between silence and complicity.

Her mantra—"History is how we see what is happening"—is both her method and her warning. In her telling, history is not past. It is precedent. And unless we learn it, we risk reliving it.

Rachel Maddow's courage is intellectual. Persistent. Scholarly. But in this age, that may be the most radical kind of bravery of all.

Washington Post Investigative Team
The Courage to Publish

The Washington Post

Democracy Dies in Darkness

Title / Role: Investigative Journalists
Term: Various
Location: United States
Education: Various
Party / Group: Independent Press

"Democracy dies in darkness."

In a time when truth itself is under siege, the Washington Post's investigative team has emerged as one of democracy's last lines of defense. Their work—methodical, relentless, often thankless—has pulled corruption, deception, and abuse of power out of the shadows and into the public square.

Investigative journalism has always been difficult. It requires months—sometimes years—of research, verification, and legal risk. But in recent years, those obstacles multiplied. Disinformation surged. Political leaders attacked the free press as "enemies of the people." Reporters became targets of harassment, digital surveillance, and even physical threats. Despite this hostile environment, the Washington Post investigative unit did not retreat. It doubled down.

Their courage was not a single headline, but a pattern of persistence. From the exposure of hidden financial dealings by elected officials, to the uncovering of election interference networks, to deep reporting on COVID-19 response failures, the Post's investigations offered citizens what no opinion column or social feed could: proof.

They dealt not in speculation, but in evidence. In documents, timelines, and accountability. Their reporting shaped congressional hearings, informed judicial inquiries, and equipped the public with facts necessary for self-governance. They were not passive observers. They were the architects of informed consent in a democracy teetering on mistrust.

The iconic phrase beneath their masthead—"Democracy dies in darkness"—is not a slogan. It is a mission. It reminds both readers and reporters that the task of journalism is not just to reflect events, but to illuminate systems of power that might otherwise operate unchecked.

The risks they faced were not abstract. Reporters were sued, subpoenaed, smeared, and in some cases, stalked. The institution itself was labeled "fake news" by powerful figures. But these journalists kept reporting—day after day, leak after leak, whistleblower after whistleblower—because the alternative was silence. And silence, in times of creeping authoritarianism, is complicity.

Their newsroom became a war room for truth. Editors shielded sources. Legal teams defended First Amendment rights. Journalists followed money, motives, and memos wherever the story led. And the result was not just journalism—it was democratic intervention.

In an era where reality can feel like narrative warfare, the Washington Post investigative team served as fact's last fortress.

Their courage was institutional, yes—but also deeply personal. Each byline represented someone who chose the long fight over the easy click. Who believed that what we know matters—and that we still have a right to know.

CHAPTER V — Political Dissent Across Ideologies

ProPublica
The Courage to Investigate

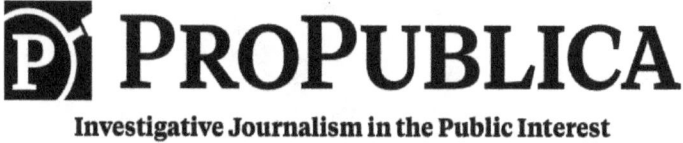

Pɔ̃ PROPUBLICA
Investigative Journalism in the Public Interest

Title / Role: Nonprofit Investigative Newsroom
Term: 2007–present
Location: United States
Education: Various
Party / Group: Independent Journalism

"Investigative journalism in the public interest."

In the age of fast takes and fleeting headlines, ProPublica chose the harder path: depth. Founded in 2007 as a nonprofit newsroom, its mission was as bold as it was idealistic — to pursue accountability journalism that serves no shareholder, no party, and no interest except the public's.

That mission has grown into one of the most powerful forces for investigative reporting in the United States.

ProPublica's courage lies not only in the stories it tells, but in the structures it exposes — the quiet systems of corruption, inequality, and unchecked power that often go ignored by commercial outlets constrained by revenue and speed. Its reporters take months, even years, to pursue a single investigation. And when the truth finally emerges, it is devastating — and irrefutable.

Its investigations have uncovered judicial conflicts of interest, failures in veterans' healthcare, racial disparities in law enforcement, and the hidden influence of billionaires over democratic institutions. Most recently, ProPublica's reporting on Supreme Court justices receiving unreported gifts sent shockwaves through the legal and political world. These revelations weren't accidents. They were the result of sustained, intentional work — of reporters following leads that others dismissed or feared.

The newsroom's nonprofit status is not a footnote. It is a philosophy. By decoupling journalism from advertising, ProPublica created a rare space where independence is not just protected but prioritized. It collaborates freely with other outlets, amplifying impact over ego. Its model challenges the notion that courage in journalism must come from lone wolves. At ProPublica, courage is collaborative.

Its motto — "Investigative journalism in the public interest" — is not decorative. It defines every editorial decision. While other newsrooms shrink under financial pressure, ProPublica invests more. While others chase virality, it pursues veracity. Its reporters write for history, not for traffic.

But courage comes with consequences. ProPublica's work often draws backlash — from powerful individuals, from political factions, from institutions that would prefer secrecy. Its journalists face lawsuits, smear campaigns, and attempted discrediting. But they persist. Because for them, truth is not an industry — it's a democratic function.

ProPublica proves that journalism, at its best, does not chase power. It checks it.

In a media ecosystem distorted by speed, bias, and financial constraint, ProPublica remains a sentinel — methodical, unafraid, and unbought. Its courage is not loud, but lasting. And for a democracy in search of accountability, that makes all the difference.

CHAPTER V — Political Dissent Across Ideologies

Liz Cheney
The Courage to Stand Against Her Party

Title / Role: U.S. Representative (Former Vice Chair, January 6 Committee)
Term: 2017–2023
Location: Wyoming
Education: BA Colorado College, JD University of Chicago
Party / Group: Republican Party

"There will come a day when Donald Trump is gone, but your dishonor will remain."

Courage, in American politics, is rarely defined by agreement. More often, it is revealed in dissent—especially when that dissent comes from within. Few modern figures embody this more fully than Liz Cheney, the conservative congresswoman from Wyoming who chose principle over power, and constitutional fidelity over political survival.

Cheney did not change parties. She did not renounce her values. What changed was her refusal to conform to a political movement that abandoned truth. As the daughter of a former vice president and a rising star in Republican leadership, Cheney could have played the game. She could have looked away, kept quiet, or softened her stance. Instead, she took the microphone—and told the truth.

Her moment of reckoning came in the aftermath of the 2020 election, as falsehoods about electoral fraud metastasized into an insurrection. While many in her party equivocated or enabled, Cheney made it clear: the attack on the U.S. Capitol was not a protest. It was a violent assault on democratic order. And silence in the face of that reality, she said, was complicity.

As Vice Chair of the House Select Committee investigating January 6, Cheney played an instrumental role in assembling the factual record, interviewing witnesses, and holding high-ranking officials to account. Her questioning was sharp. Her tone was resolute. She did not posture or grandstand—she prosecuted the truth.

The cost was swift and personal. She was censured by her state party. Removed from Republican leadership. Targeted by Donald Trump himself. Eventually, she lost her seat in Congress. But she did not lose her purpose. Cheney made clear that her oath—to the Constitution, not a party—was nonnegotiable.

In many ways, Cheney's courage is paradoxical: a conservative defending democracy from within a party she still identifies with, even as it rejected her. But that is what makes it profound. She showed that dissent is not betrayal. It can be the highest form of loyalty—loyalty to something larger than faction or ambition.

Her now-famous quote—"There will come a day when Donald Trump is gone, but your dishonor will remain"—was not just a condemnation. It was a challenge. To every lawmaker, voter, and institution tempted by convenience over courage.

Liz Cheney stood nearly alone. But in that solitude, she clarified the stakes. She reminded the country that democracy is not protected by unanimity. It is protected by conscience.

John Bolton
The Courage to Dissent After Power

Title / Role: National Security
Advisor/Ambassador
Term: 2018–2019
Location: United States
Education: BA Yale University, JD
Yale Law School
Party / Group: Republican Party

"The Constitution comes first."

John Bolton was not an icon of resistance. He was, for much of his career, its antithesis—a hawkish enforcer of executive authority, a fixture in Republican foreign policy circles, and an unapologetic believer in American hard power. That is what made his eventual dissent all the more striking.

Bolton served as National Security Advisor under President Donald Trump, an appointment welcomed by many conservatives. But within months, the tensions between Bolton's worldview and the President's style—impulsive, personalized, and transactional—became irreconcilable. Bolton, steeped in institutional rigor, found himself confronting a White House where loyalty was valued over legality, and ideology over process.

When he left office in 2019, he did not immediately speak out. But what followed marked a rare moment of internal dissent from one of the most ideologically aligned members of the administration. In his 2020 memoir, The Room Where It

Happened, Bolton pulled back the curtain on a presidency that, in his view, subordinated national security to personal interest.

This was not mere criticism. It was an insider's indictment—from someone who had held immense power, now willing to dismantle the mythologies he had once helped construct. His disclosures added critical detail to the growing body of evidence around the misuse of presidential authority, and though his critics pointed to the timing of his revelations, the weight of what he said could not be ignored.

What took courage in Bolton's dissent was not just that it broke ranks—it broke expectations. He was not a liberal, not a moderate, and certainly not someone seeking approval from the political left. His allegiance was to the machinery of statecraft, to institutional norms forged through decades of governance. And when he saw those norms endangered by a cult of personality, he chose to speak.

He was denounced as disloyal by some, opportunistic by others. But in a political climate where so few insiders dared to break from the gravitational pull of party loyalty, Bolton's refusal to remain silent was an act of integrity, however belated.

His statement—"The Constitution comes first"—is not dramatic. But for someone who operated in the heart of executive power, it is revolutionary. It asserts that even the strongest defenders of authority must draw the line when that authority forgets its source.

John Bolton's dissent did not stem from ideology, but from principle. And in moments of democratic stress, that kind of dissent is not only rare—it is essential.

CHAPTER VI — Grassroots and Civic Movements

Indivisible
The Courage to Organize

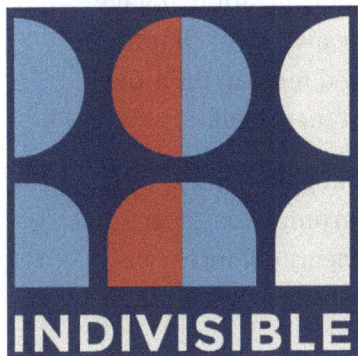

Title / Role: Civic Movement
Term: 2016–present
Location: United States
Education / Background:
Grassroots organizers
Party / Group: Progressive Civic
Movement

"Democracy requires participation."

Indivisible was born not in a political war room, but in a Google Doc—shared among friends, former congressional staffers, and ordinary Americans who sensed that something precious was slipping away after the 2016 election. What began as a guide—a practical, no-frills handbook for resisting authoritarian drift—quickly became a movement. And from that urgency came one of the most impactful examples of grassroots civic courage in modern American history.

Unlike traditional political campaigns, Indivisible wasn't built around a single candidate or issue. It was built around process: how to organize, how to apply pressure, how to use democratic tools to resist democratic erosion. The group's founders understood something many missed—that the real battle for democracy would not be fought at the top, but in town halls, local offices, and under-attended hearings where accountability either begins or dies.

The courage of Indivisible lies in its radical decentralization. It gave power away. It empowered people to form their own local chapters, plan their own actions, and decide what mattered most in their own communities. In doing so, it democratized resistance itself.

From its earliest actions—flooding congressional phone lines, organizing protests outside offices, mobilizing around healthcare and voting rights—Indivisible made one thing clear: democracy is not self-maintaining. It requires sweat, repetition, and collective effort.

And it requires moral clarity. While some political groups watered down language to broaden appeal, Indivisible did not equivocate. It named authoritarian threats when it saw them. It recognized white nationalism as a danger. It understood voter suppression not as strategy, but as theft.

By 2018, Indivisible chapters had helped shift congressional races, reframe national debates, and create a civic infrastructure that rivaled established institutions. But more important than any single election win was the culture it helped cultivate—a culture where ordinary citizens once again saw themselves as part of the political process, not merely subjects to its consequences.

Its courage is quiet, collective, and persistent. It is found in the volunteers knocking doors in the rain, in retirees learning how to speak at public meetings, in young organizers challenging disinformation with facts and empathy. These are not the heroic moments that make headlines, but they are the habits that sustain a republic.

"Democracy requires participation." It sounds simple. But in a time when apathy is rewarded and cynicism monetized, showing up is an act of defiance. Indivisible has turned that defiance into a democratic force.

AMERICAN CIVIL LIBERTIES UNION (ACLU)
The Courage of Litigation as Democratic Defense

ACLU

Title / Role: Civic and Legal
Organization
Term: 1920–present
Location: United States
Education / Background:
Constitutional law, civil liberties
litigation
Party / Group: Nonpartisan legal
advocacy

"Rights do not defend themselves."

Not every defense of democracy is loud. Some take place in court filings, injunctions, and 3 a.m. rulings that stop planes from taking off. When democratic norms are threatened at scale, courage sometimes looks less like speeches—and more like lawsuits. For over a century, the American Civil Liberties Union (ACLU) has embodied that form of institutional courage, standing between executive overreach and constitutional principle with relentless legal precision.

The ACLU's strength lies not just in what it defends, but in how quickly it moves. Within days of the 2017 executive order banning travelers from several Muslim-majority countries, the ACLU filed lawsuits in federal courts, secured emergency injunctions, and deployed lawyers to airports across the country. In a moment when chaos reigned, they imposed order—not through politics, but through law.

Their courage is rarely cinematic. It is procedural. Tireless. Often anonymous. ACLU attorneys and affiliates are vilified by cable news panels, harassed online, and targeted by political leaders who prefer power unchallenged. Yet they persist—unmoved by popularity, guided only by constitutional fidelity.

They have challenged:

- Voter suppression laws cloaked in claims of election security
- Abortion restrictions meant to deny autonomy
- Protest crackdowns disguised as public safety
- Surveillance overreach passed in the name of security
- Partisan manipulation of the Department of Justice

And when they file suit, it is not performance. It is preservation.

ACLU litigation does not just slow democratic erosion—it often halts it outright. Injunctions they secure keep polling places open, prevent unlawful detentions, or block enforcement of unconstitutional laws until the courts can act. These legal actions create time—time for democracy to catch its breath, to function, to defend itself.

Their model is institutional courage: a nationwide structure of expertise, built to act fast and absorb the blowback. They litigate not just for headlines, but for precedent. For the millions of Americans who cannot afford legal defense, the ACLU becomes the firewall between government power and personal freedom.

"Rights do not defend themselves."

That belief underpins every motion filed, every brief argued, every hearing attended.

In an age when executive authority expands and disinformation clouds the law, the ACLU reminds us that the Constitution is not ornamental. It is enforceable—if someone insists on its relevance. And they do.

Their courage doesn't seek celebration. It seeks protection. For immigrants caught in legal limbo. For protestors threatened by unlawful arrests. For patients turned away from clinics. For voters facing barriers meant to silence their voice. The ACLU fights not just for abstract rights, but for lived dignity.

They are not politicians or pundits. But their legacy is vast. When future generations ask how democracy endured during moments of stress, they will find the ACLU's name in the footnotes—in case law, injunctions, and decisions that proved the rule of law was still a line worth defending.

In short: they didn't just react to threats. They sued them.

CHAPTER VII — Culture, Sports, and Moral Leadership

Colin Kaepernick
The Courage to Protest

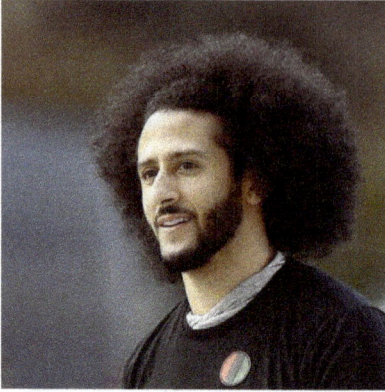

Title / Role: Professional
Athlete, Activist
Term: 2016–present
Location: United States
Education: Some college –
University of Nevada
Party / Group: Independent

"Believe in something, even if it costs everything."

Courage sometimes kneels. And in that kneeling, it can change a nation.

In 2016, during the playing of the national anthem before a preseason NFL game, quarterback Colin Kaepernick made a decision that would alter the trajectory of his life—and ignite one of the most divisive debates in modern American culture. He took a knee. Quietly. Respectfully. Unapologetically.

It was not a protest against the anthem itself, or the military, or the flag. It was a protest against police brutality, racial injustice, and a country that too often asked for the silence of the oppressed in exchange for the comfort of the majority. The act was symbolic, but the message was searing: justice in America is not yet equal, and until it is, silence is complicity.

The backlash was immediate and ferocious. Kaepernick was vilified, misquoted, and misunderstood. Politicians called for his firing. Fans burned his jersey. He was, for all intents and purposes, blackballed from the NFL. No team would sign him again.

But Kaepernick did not flinch. He understood what he was risking. In fact, he counted on it. His sacrifice—his career, his livelihood—was the cost of his statement. And it is that cost that turned a single act of protest into a movement.

Over time, others followed. Athletes in nearly every sport, from high school to professional leagues, took a knee. What began with one man on a sideline became a visual vocabulary for dissent—a way to say, "We see injustice. We refuse to pretend it isn't there."

Kaepernick's protest forced institutions to react. The NFL, once complicit in his silencing, later acknowledged it had mishandled his message. National conversations about race, policing, and patriotism began to shift, not because they were new, but because they could no longer be ignored.

His courage was not performative. He didn't monetize it, didn't retract it, didn't reposition it to win favor. He stood in the storm—and stayed there. He funded legal defense for victims of police violence. He launched a Know Your Rights campaign to educate young people on their power. He continued to speak, even when speaking closed doors.

Critics asked why an athlete would protest. The better question is: why not? In a country where celebrity often buys silence, Kaepernick chose truth. He didn't do what was easy, or popular, or brand-safe. He did what was right.

His kneel was quiet. But it echoed across stadiums, into courtrooms, classrooms, and boardrooms. It revealed the enduring tension between patriotism and dissent—and reminded the country that those two are not opposites. They are, in fact, inseparable.

Colin Kaepernick did not set out to be a symbol. But in risking everything for something greater, he became one.

Megan Rapinoe
The Courage to Demand Equality

Title / Role: Professional
Athlete and Advocate
Term: 2012–present
Location: United States
Education: BA University of
Portland
Party / Group: Independent

"You cannot win without equality."

In sports, courage is often measured in goals, in last-second victories, in physical risk. But Megan Rapinoe showed that true athletic courage can also mean stepping off the field—and using the spotlight not just to shine, but to illuminate injustice.

A World Cup champion, Olympic gold medalist, and global icon of women's soccer, Rapinoe's impact transcends her athletic record. Her legacy is built not only on what she did with the ball, but what she did with her voice.

Her fight for equal pay began not with a press release, but with a principle: that excellence deserves equity. As one of the most decorated players in U.S. soccer history, she knew firsthand how vast the disparities were between the men's and women's national teams—not just in paychecks, but in training conditions, travel support, media coverage, and institutional respect.

Rather than accept it, she challenged it. Alongside her teammates, Rapinoe led legal and public campaigns demanding equal compensation for equal work. It was not a stunt. It was a demand rooted in labor rights, justice, and the value of women's contributions—not just in sports, but in society.

She faced backlash. Dismissal. Mockery. Critics labeled her arrogant, political, divisive. But Rapinoe responded with what she has always wielded best: clarity. Her statements were bold, but never reckless. She spoke not only as an athlete, but as a citizen—about race, gender, sexuality, and the power structures that shape opportunity.

Openly gay, Rapinoe also became one of the most prominent LGBTQ+ advocates in international sports. Her visibility mattered. For countless fans, especially young ones, she offered a model of authenticity and pride at the highest level of achievement. She didn't separate her activism from her career. She fused them.

Her decision to kneel during the national anthem in solidarity with Colin Kaepernick was another chapter in that courage. In doing so, she connected racial justice to gender equality, refusing to silo one fight from another. Her protest was not performative—it was a recognition that all liberation is linked.

But perhaps her greatest power lies in her refusal to become bitter. Even when institutions pushed back—even when change came slowly—Rapinoe's message remained rooted in joy, conviction, and belief in progress. She celebrated as fiercely as she criticized. She made justice not only urgent, but aspirational.

"You cannot win without equality," she said. Not just on the scoreboard, but in the world we build around it.

Megan Rapinoe is not just a player. She is a force—a reminder that sports are never separate from society, and that sometimes the bravest thing a champion can do is speak.

REFERENCES

American Civil Liberties Union. (2017–2024). Federal litigation archive. https://www.aclu.org

American Civil Liberties Union. (2020). Supreme Court and federal injunction filings. https://www.aclu.org

Associated Press. (2023). Georgia prosecutor brings historic election interference case. https://apnews.com

Brennan Center for Justice. (2020). Congressional oversight and the rule of law. https://www.brennancenter.org

Cheney, L. (2023). Oath and honor. Little, Brown and Company.

Chicago Tribune. (2023). Pritzker's equity agenda and democratic governance. https://www.chicagotribune.com

Council on Foreign Relations. (2021). McMaster on strategic competence and truth. https://www.cfr.org

Fulton County District Attorney's Office. (2023). State of Georgia v. Trump et al.: Indictment. https://fultoncountyga.gov

Giffords Law Center. (2023). Mark Kelly and the fight for gun safety. https://giffords.org

Goldberg, J. (2020). James Mattis: In union there is strength. The Atlantic. https://www.theatlantic.com

Holder, E. (2022). Our unfinished march: The violent past and imperiled future of the vote. One World.

Indivisible. (2017). Indivisible: A practical guide for resisting the Trump agenda. https://www.indivisible.org

John F. Kennedy Presidential Library and Museum. (n.d.). Profile in Courage Award: Nancy Pelosi. https://www.jfklibrary.org

Los Angeles Times. (2022). Newsom's pandemic leadership and the recall election. https://www.latimes.com

Maddow, R. (2023). Prequel: An American fight against fascism. Crown.

Mattis, J. (2019). Call sign chaos: Learning to lead. Random House.

McFaul, M. (2018). From Cold War to hot peace. Houghton Mifflin Harcourt.

McMaster, H. R. (2020). Battlegrounds: The fight to defend the free world. Harper.

National Constitution Center. (2021). Judicial independence in a time of political pressure. https://constitutioncenter.org

New York State Office of the Attorney General. (2024). Attorney General James secures landmark judgment for fraud. https://ag.ny.gov

New York State Office of the Attorney General. (2024). People of the State of New York v. Trump et al. Court filings and judgments. https://ag.ny.gov

New York Times. (2018). How Indivisible became a grassroots powerhouse. https://www.nytimes.com

Office of the Governor of California. (2021). Executive orders and public health directives. https://www.gov.ca.gov

Office of the Governor of Illinois. (2024). Legislative and executive actions. https://www.illinois.gov

Oyez Project. (2024). Supreme Court case summaries. https://www.oyez.org

ProPublica. (2016–2024). Investigative reporting archive. https://www.propublica.org

Pulitzer Prize Board. (n.d.). ProPublica award citations. https://www.pulitzer.org

Stanford Freeman Spogli Institute. (2023). McFaul on democracy and authoritarianism. https://fsi.stanford.edu

Supreme Court of the United States. (2016–2024). Slip opinions and dissents. https://www.supremecourt.gov

Support and Defend the Constitution. (2021). Open letter from retired senior military officers. https://www.flagofficers4america.com

Texas Tribune. (2024). Jasmine Crockett emerges as a leading Democratic voice on democracy. https://www.texastribune.org

United States Courts. (2017–2021). Selected federal court opinions. https://www.uscourts.gov

United States Department of Justice. (2015). Voting Rights Act enforcement records. https://www.justice.gov

United States House of Representatives. (2022). Final report of the Select Committee to investigate the January 6th attack on the United States Capitol. U.S. Government Publishing Office.

United States House Permanent Select Committee on Intelligence. (2019). Report on Russian active measures campaigns and interference in the 2016 U.S. election. https://intelligence.house.gov

United States Senate. (2020). National security testimony. https://www.senate.gov

United States Senate. (2024). Official biography and legislative record. https://www.senate.gov

Washington Post. (2016–2024). Investigative reporting archive. https://www.washingtonpost.com

Washington Post. (2021). Former generals warn against obeying illegal orders. https://www.washingtonpost.com

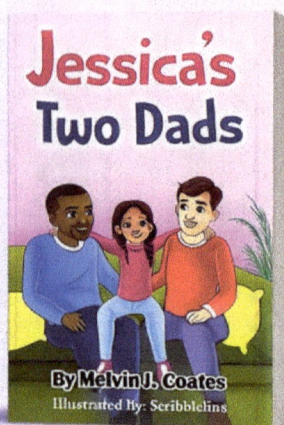

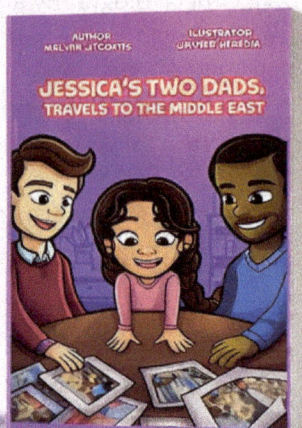

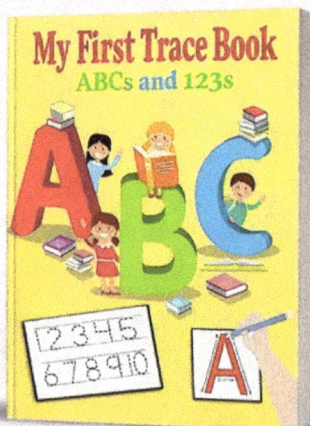

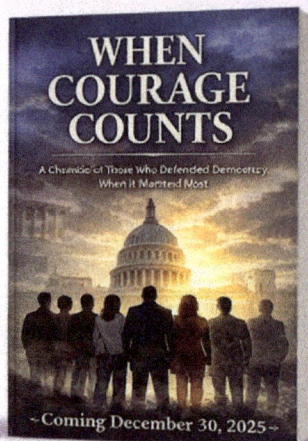

www.ingramcontent.com/pod-product-compliance
Lightning Source LLC
Chambersburg PA
CBHW070029030426
42335CB00017B/2347

* 9 7 8 1 9 5 6 0 8 8 1 3 7 *